T0166417

Andrew Faulkner

Need Machine

Coach House Books, Toronto

Canada Council   Conseil des Arts    ONTARIO ARTS COUNCIL   Canada
for the Arts   du Canada   CONSEIL DES ARTS DE L'ONTARIO

Published with the generous assistance of the Canada Council for the Arts
and the Ontario Arts Council. Coach House Books also acknowledges the
support of the Government of Canada through the Canada Book Fund and
the Government of Ontario through the Ontario Book Publishing Tax Credit.

LIBRARY AND ARCHIVES CANADA CATALOGUING IN PUBLICATION

Faulkner, Andrew, 1984-
        Need machine / Andrew Faulkner.

Issued also in electronic format.
ISBN 978-1-55245-275-2

        I. Title.

PS8611.A85N44 2013   C811'.6   C2013-900224-3

Need Machine is available as an ebook: ISBN 978 1 77056 343 8.

for Leigh

TRUMPETS ON MUTE

As if a kidnapper slunk off with sound
in a burlap sack. The ransom note:
sheet music for 'Taps' scratched into a vinyl 45.
These are the trumpets we like. We turn
the static up and roll the top down.
Let's do doughnuts inside the compound.

Deep concern shows itself in funny ways:
the faces of most sitcom actors.
We've been cruelly typecast for years.
April is a versatile name and easy to spell.
We say, *Out, devil*, with conviction.
Valve, stem of music, better intentions

on video loop. In dog years, we've aged
considerably. In the computer age,
we're already obsolete. The Real
spends a lot of time on the DL.
We never tire of the banana-peel skit.
When we say, *Out, devil*, we totally mean it.

RATS

In the walls, running along pipes
like a mob of white blood cells.
Sometimes things aren't okay.
Rats in the pantry, the kitchen
of the mind. Rats in the mortgage, rats alive
and scurrying like a renewed fear of death.
Long in the teeth, long in need.
The change-purse hearts of rats under the floorboard.
Rats in the upper tier of the stadium, peering
over the railing, rats raining down
on the field. Rats in the maize, the long grass.
Rats underfoot, rats descending from overhead
like it's Baghdad, 1999, and there's oil to be had.
Rats the necessary gears in the mower.
Rats only one or two removes from us –
that is, they're delicate and obnoxious
and consist mostly of water. Hanover rat,
brown rat, sewer rat, brush its shoulder off
because a rat's a pimp too. Norwegian rat,
water rat, rats always the missing multiplier.
Researcher John Calhoun built a perfect, rat-sized
studio apartment and the rats he leased it to
drew and redrew themselves over generations
until they more or less evaporated.
Wharf rat, Old World rat. 'RATS': worth a whopping
four points, though given a random assortment
of 100 tiles, it could occur again and again and again.
Can you imagine playing with rats your whole life
and then, like Calhoun, being asked to meet the pope?
But Pope Paul VI was old by then and no longer steely
or spring-loaded. So while you consider rats,
with their glass-eyed guts that never shut,
don't forget the rest of us poor unblinking sinners.

THE LOBBY

The Holiday Inn sign issues the kind of light
you inhale through a dollar bill.

On the fringe of the parking lot, it's a lot like
the Wild West: a grave Corolla rusts,

and someone pisses on an oak at dusk
as if his urine were an axe.

I commission a new scent to enter
rooms before me and pat down its occupants,

confiscating cellphones and sketch pads.
It's not paranoia if your interest is academic.

I'm flannel-mouthed. Produce a sweat that lingers
like a waxy second skin. In the corner, the last American-made

pinball machine grazes on quarters.
But the concierge doesn't care. His yawn is wide and full

as a luscious lash arcing over the eye of finance.
That's a mouthful, over the phone. *Can you say that again?*

The piped-in music swells like teen acne.
The concierge nods solemnly. He can, he can.

ICE CREAM WEATHER

Two coffees deep into Sunday. Cut flowers
a little wilted, *désolé*. Subscribers' attention
lather-whipped by a crossword

for an hour, maybe two, then the mind,
which is its own beast, trots off
to a corner and licks its genitals.

Deft as an ASM-114 Hellfire, that stalwart
of air-to-surface missiles, the radio
inserts a hook in the lip. The July sweats

are at it again. I know what you're thinking
and that's not it. The air conditioner
with its idiot whirr locks silence

in the closet. If it's good
maybe it can come out later
and we can all have ice cream.

DON'T FORGET TENT PEGS

Low, stubbled hills. My boots
sweep the brush.
The air kicked like a dog.
When birds perch on a slipstream
I think, *I know what animal I am.*

I've made an orange scrub-scoured
tent my home. At night, shadows rise
like Whac-A-Moles and when they do
I name them what they are: orange
porcupine, jar of orange pencils, shrub.

In the tent, I'm an island and everything on it:
Mosquitos. Dead citrus tree. Lemonade
stand. A long-beached whale

repurposed as a hut. At times I step in and wear
the bones like skin. Except they're bones,
and when it rains I wonder where it is
my skin has gone. Is this what it's like
to be wet inside?

WING

The east wing of my heart rises like a hot
air balloon. The west wing descends like bad
news on the oblivious. The radical wing
of my heart sets fire to the stock exchange.
The silent wing gestures like a museum.
The wings of hope trade away several promising prospects.
Winging it at the press conference,
despair tells fans the team wouldn't
have made the playoffs anyway. As a right-winger
I've scored several goals and lowered
your taxes. As a left-winger, I'm here for you.
Attention all passengers, this is the captain speaking:
that thing on the wing is the old god, the small god,
all the thieves and lawyers, every good deal you've made.
Ladies and gentlemen, this is what keeps us aloft.

MODERN LOVE

I passed, lonely as a damaged package
in a discount bin, through a number
of difficult months. I couldn't roll
my windows down or get a seat at brunch.

I took the high road, back streets,
stuck to shops in the mezzanine.
But the switch that toggles my factory settings
is a finger loitering between a door

and its frame, caught between 'delight'
and 'just missed an 80%-off sale.' My tongue grazed
like an ATV, and then you sidled up like an IED.
I'm on my hands and where my knees used to be.

According to my horoscope,
love is a thug with piano wire.
I've strapped dynamite to your heart
and jammed a bit between your teeth.

How bored you must have been
before you met me.

RUSTBUCKET IN A FIELD WITH FLOWERS

The glitzy thing must have hauled itself
to the far side of the ditch and rolled over
like a pregnant dog about to burst.
Once described as *zippy* by salesmen
who use *German* as an adjective.
As a minor roadside attraction it has its charm:
cottage-bound families let their cameras
jaw at the hull. A squat bunker
that rain lugs into its rust years.
In the back seat, running on fumes,
field mice fuck like teenagers.
The glove compartment's loosened maw
is a small bed for a clutch of heather.
It's been standing at the road's doorbell
for what must be years, a rough and unexpected
bouquet thrust briefly into a skeptical life.
A mechanical bull that, in a stunning reversal,
hogties you with awe.
But it's what people want: flowers.

CHORUS

'The hour is an enormous eye.
Inside it, we come and go like reflections.'
                              – Octavio Paz

Welcome to Toronto, on whose craggy beaches
the Argonauts land, and lose, and repeat.
Sweat in a brow of Astroturf, Astroturf a cold cloth
pressed to the forehead of a fevered hour.
Are we sometimes frigid with envy? Exactly, actually.

I'm here. Ahem. I'm ready. Last night a friend was married
in the echo of a rental hall in Scarborough and I celebrated
by cultivating a slow headache. On the dance floor I swayed
in the great electric light of four-four time. In an earlier hour,
there were three of me: me with the untied tie,

me in the mirror, left-handed, wielding the tie like a cudgel,
and me in the eye of the hour trying to figure out the tie's
secret handshake. Toronto the Half-dressed, the Business Casual.
I'm not the first to say this but an hour isn't enough.
And then the hour coming to a close,

always closing like a salesman, by the bucketload,
by the pailful. Our skylights, our hatchet-like bylaws.
The timber of our ambition. This morning the QEW
is a meadow of cars in which I lay my headache down,
traffic limping like a waitress working a double in a cast.

Which isn't to say there's not money in pockets,
obviously by Bay, and in the hills and parks and echoing
like the subway cars shuttling folks from hour to hour,
the underground life, crumpled transfer in a pocket.
I'm here. I'm ready for my costume, my ridiculous prop,

the walk-on scene by the fountain. I'm in relief
like the conclusion of a pregnancy scare.
Oh, what could have been, in an hour made
and unmade, bloodless as an insurance claim.
City of equivocation, Great Equivocator by the Lake,

Toronto the Retailer, the Beast from the East, Middle Finger
to Western Sensibilities. Toronto: whole hog, gassed up
and living better by living in a condo. This little hour
antiqued on Queen St., this little hour drank O'Keefe's.
And this little city from block to block, from hour to hour.

It's not that I don't like the slump and drag of Sherbourne and Dundas,
the slow exodus to Forest Hill, Richmond Hill, Vaughan Mills.
When grandparents die we bury their bones and leave.
It's not that I don't like the concrete tomb where the Blue Jays play,
the days' earlier hours when I pilot towards lunch

or the afternoon's flashy bits of circumstance that steer me home.
As if in the naming we could make a thing: Rosebank Dr., Progress Ave.,
ash in the mouth. The hour a cadaver on which we practice
and practice again. It's the Hour of Being Hauled to Attention
at the Corner of Bloor and Wherever; someone's just been hit

by a car, and for the feeling of his feet aloft, above him
in the hour's air, he thanks the driver by introducing a fist
to the car's windshield. In these ways do we bridge the gaps
between us. Hour with a worm in its molar, with mud on the mudflap.
At our feet the evening gathers like litter,

a hot little mess spied in the hour's mirrored eye.
And around each corner another wildfire of strangers,
insistent as a commercial break: we're here,
we're burning up, come find us.

YOUNG LIBERALS

There's so much I want
to do. No, serious – fearlessly
stick my bronzed head
into a photograph's wide jaw,
for example. That's leadership.
You can really trust someone
who does that, and I want
to be trusted. People love people
who build roads, and love
is the greatest virtue of all.
St. Augustine said that
before he was fed to lions,
lions that appraised him with the eye
of their throat and found him wanting.
But appetites are not to be ignored –
not when they're so logical,
and not when campaign buttons
come so cheap. I'll start where I start,
but given the bulk discounts,
why not go for it all. Just think of it –
trust and love and, failing that,
at least one of the two.
Here, let me get a pin for you.
The pleasure's all mine.

♥

If you can't hear the sound of a heart,
half-buried, grinding like a pulp mill
then try a stethoscope. In one valve
and out the other, as the textbooks say.
A capacity for sadness is an incredible letdown.
I'd rather see the whole litter
of puppies neutered and be done with it –

where was I going with that?
I told you I get lost in low light.
Cute little thing with your use of both hands,
help me finish this off. Puppies:
you can't take them to the museum,
no matter how much the kids plead.
Just imagine the bones they'll drag home.

I THINK IT JUST MOVED

They've been digging in the backyard again.
Like a cavity, the ground near the fence
has opened wide. From the kitchen window
something was spotted: a sky-blue promise,
a flirtation, an *x*.
                    The world is full of people
who get their teeth pulled. The world is full
of people who pray to odds, who close their eyes
when they sign. There are several other things
I would like to tell you, but not here.

There are rumours of gold, rumours
of a French maid buried somewhere near the compost.
In the moonlight you can see her garter belt,
so lacy a man could curl up in it and sleep.

They've been digging. The first one to tear a strip
off her thigh-high skirt and make a flag of it wins.

HIT AND RUN

Swing a hefty wrench against a hollow pipe.
The result sort of sounds like *foul*.
This sort of thought can fill a lifetime.
It can also occupy hours while high.
Approximate Major League action everywhere!
Let the toilet run and swing away. Like dusk
lurking in the corners of a room, higher minds
are unwilling to focus on anything in particular.
The fun I've had robbed me blind.

LIKE LIONS

we mostly slept.
Lounged on the stripmall's runway,
little concrete villa, all aluminum sides
and neon light. So pretty in the dark.
Thin-lipped weather in the plaza's shallow avenues
with its low curbs and garbage cans of different sizes.
We all shook hands and grinned.

She invited me over, or I her; the details
are whitewashed with style. We hung around,
dim and cool like a bunker before the war.
Practiced taking our clothes off
in a silence crisp as a pressed suit.
Thumbed the buttons on the shirt
of the room around us. We took big gulps.

Like a trust fund, we became more luxurious
with each passing day. Certainty fanned out
like a search team. A general consensus wavered,
broke, re-collected itself. Things got boring
and one of us left. With apologies to those of you
waiting for the payoff, I guess this is it.

HANSARD

The unacknowledged legislators of this evening's meal
insist we acknowledge our sources in the grandest style.
They insist that when we grow up we become narrative poems.
I've dined beneath Roman arches in a lightning storm.

I've dined by the banks of the Arno, the Tiber, by three
creeks you've never heard of. There are several other
meals I could tell you about while we're here.

My belly swells with the music courtesy of SiriusXM
Satellite Radio. Courtesy of modern plumbing,
your water glass is filled. The unacknowledged legislators

would like you to tip 15%. They would like
you to return the cutlery. The unacknowledged legislators
would like to thank Hollywood Records for the appearance
of Miley Cyrus, who will be checking your purse at the exit.

SYNDICATION

Lassoed by one of those syndicated afternoons.
If you want to get poetic about it, I was bound,
gagged and leashed by the soft light of *Cheers*,
Sam, Woody and the gang playing a game
of Twenty Questions with me Abu Ghraib-style.
Mostly, I wore boxers, through which
I attended to dry skin. After *Seinfield*,
Law & Order. I could go on.

During the commercials I hear a night court of mice
in the walls, scratching and alive; gavels clap
as they conduct awful trials *in camera*.

LITTLE MISS HALTON REGION

I confess to having cried in a legion hall
as the local rag's reporter/photographer point-formed
my reaction to the indecency of being called *runner-up*.
I confess to this reaction being anger at, among others,
other contestants' parents, though they were guilty
only of an overzealous pride despite their children
finishing several removes from the 'LITTLE MISS
HALTON REGION BEAUTY QUEEN' sash.
I acknowledge giving over to a grief that was swirling
and sharp, and the locus of pain was obvious –
Debbie Miller, who smiles like a hood ornament
and smells like peppermint schnapps.
I confess to the greater part of my anguish burning
like a tire fire, which is to say in the months that followed
I considered awful Debbie in ways that could be described
as *detailed* or *criminal*, but however you classify
these thoughts, they were without a doubt scaly and prehensile.
And I confess to understanding the relevance
of the phrase *put out to pasture* in its relation
to the Platonic ideal of a capital-H Horse,
and now admit to the flimsy laws that govern our talents
and the evaluations thereof, namely, how in the moment's
I'm-rubber-you're-glue equation I was what's led into an Elmer's factory.
Mostly, I confess to visiting a certain vehicle
in the McDonald's parking lot while Debbie sat inside
and watched her boyfriend eat, and what I did then
was a study in contrast regarding a box cutter
and a rear right tire, and all of a sudden I got old real quick,
wielded that knife like a rough dollar-store comb,
and while considering what to do next, the moon,
in an effort to describe the world the way my painstakingly
straightened hair described the asphalt,
bled generously on my innocent scalp.

SMOKING INDOORS

Hooks empty. A shed of bent sheet metal.
The sun tweaks your brain's stub, flicks it,
and a bylaw arm wrestles with a head full of splinters.
Given the chance to ignore the elbow
lifted from the table, most do.

We do what we think we need to.
Fingers printed with yellow ink, a fake tan
nicotine drew. A cigarette's papery rope unravelled.
One headlight, weaving hand to mouth.
Smoke half, butt the other half out.

TUMOUR

Little tumour, you're a blip
on the radar, corner of the body

dust is swept in. If a mirror
took negatives, archived them

in a blender and let it dry – that would be you.
Indifferent continent where metaphors go:

zebra mussel, surgeon's golf ball,
a connect-the-dots dot.

Death on a rusty tricycle.
Claustrophobe, you ask for a little light –

lungs open like a pair of hands attached to a kid
at the beach, open-palmed, saying, *Look what I found*.

AT HAND

Think of life as taking a bath.
We end up pickled and cold.
Think of gravity as taking a bath:
it's hard to stand without slipping.
Think of gravity as gravy,

that urge to smother yourself in it.
It's after dinner and your uncle
has loosened his pants by the light

of the football game on TV.
A vague shame circulates
like a draft. Grab what's at hand.
Think of professional sports
as a simile: there are so many
teams, they're so damn likeable.

HOT MESS

It is noon in the sweat glands of the gorgeous
and the pheromones are doing their thing.

But we are hungover and have to work in an hour.
And you're a tall drink of water because we're so fucking thirsty,

as lonely and out of reach as a balloon beached on the ceiling.
Dear heart, tensored by spandex, uttering a saint's lament,
shiny side of a dime in the corner of a pickpocket's eye. Well then.

The boiler room has sprung a leak and it's getting hot
in here. We could click the like button on you all day.

LOREM IPSUM

Here on the island of umbrella drinks
we make our own fun. Cocktails at three,

cocktails at four, etc., with real fruit in the drinks,
real plastic instead of glass. Pull out that ruler
and draw me something straight-ish, won't you?

This is about grief, as it is, empty as a storm-haloed beach.
It's a wonderful button that holds your shirt tightly.

From this room full of different-sized drawers
I can hear the sound of torrid fucking next door;

it's not the motion of the ocean, as they say in the biz,
but the belly of the whale you're in.

TAKING THE FUN OUT OF FUNCTION

It was the season of car alarms. Things ached
to get out. Things crawled from one hole
to another. When brushed against,
things scurried into bloom.

Of the decade, thick as coleslaw,
I think we can say, *better luck next time.*

But who needs luck when what's out there smells
like cherries and sunscreen, urine and Tic Tacs.

It was the season of visiting the mechanic.
Sugar crawled out from the fuel lines;
the wheels didn't come off, they restructured.
Of the one-liner, I think we can say, *get the fuck out.*
That's what the one-liner wants,
it wants to get out.

THAT'S WHAT SHE SAID

The morning torches your face with a new crease;
if you've been up all night, you'll know what I mean.
In the brush country of your skull a butterfly flexes
and you wake up hard-pressed to say why.

My stomach has invented several new knots
and named them all after you. I'm so happy
I could burst into flames. That's what she said.
Falling asleep is like climbing a tall, leafy tree.
The branches get narrower – spot me.

LIKE CLOCKWORK

This in drudgery, like a cold lightning-bolted
to your immune system. When playing
tennis with your desires, whose knees
do you take a crowbar to? Anapest, Budapest,
vintage crabgrass makes bad lemonade.
Looking back, there are clearly three muddy
prints: one-legged invisible dog,
do you smell something burning?

Let's waltz through this mess of a mess
together and if someone says, *Excuse me,*
Ms. Harding, your triple Axel is no good here,
you'll be speechless. But it's okay,
the vagaries you've been toting
around in your high school gym bag
have been saying it for years.

XO

There you are, skinny as the day's first hour.
And here I am, stalking you like the breeze
hunting picnickers in the summer grass.
What I'm trying to say is, it's clear
this isn't working. You think of us as *xo*.
I think of us as a three-act drama
starring a small child and a jar of aspirin.

Under the bright stage lights, it's like
you're not even here. And then I'm ushered
to my seat. Twinkle in the pilot's eye,
twinkle on the wing. Think of it as the new style
of living: we come and go in the reflection
of a heart monitor's flatline. How swell.
You should really put some ice on that.

THIS TIME WITH FEELING

Another night in the gator pond,
quick splash, the plush of it,
the flurry of hands – not your own –
it's a pleasure to meet you, it's a real

pleasure. A common theme runs through
the night like a streaker. We strain
for a glimpse then look away.
We're all tied up with nowhere to go.
In bars, boys yell, *Show us your tits!*
and girls say, *No!* World of soft
bodies, world without in/out privileges,

I dedicate this year to grief, the next
to mild contentment. I dedicate
these two hours to a tub of ice cream
and wrestling reruns.

A flu-like sentiment hangs over us
like a hung jury, staid and pleading –
Salvation Army tin, no, collection plate,
no, the plated voice of Collections: *I know,*
I know, just send us what you can.

MEAN MATT

He grew up in the woods without a lake in sight.
His mother was a hellcat and his father was an itch.

What's good is rarely *good*.

His Kmart aesthetic is infectious – he comes over once
and your curtains are floral patterned and stained for weeks.
Always flushes so you don't know what was there.

He's a slow waltz with a gorgeous someone across a floor of tacks.
Loves like a Brillo pad. Attentive as an empty fridge.

And what, exactly, did you expect?

He labours through rain season, mud season,
sailing a sharp-blue kite through the middle of the night.

This is what we think of when clouds appear.

Once worked as a dentist on an oil rig. He's what's
fresh rust and what's dried blood.

But he's good at what he does.

Sees daughters as spare parts, sons as useless legislation.
Watches our sisters from a webcam no one knows is there.

It's always our fault for not knowing better.

He has a bulldog's jaw, the heart of an old engine.
And here he is singing a song of apology

for arriving late to your birthday party.
He brought a present, and his intentions are as clear
as a sliver of glass in chocolate cake.

This will only be hard on one of you. Guess who?

FOUND: THE SMELL OF GAS

A case can be made
for bookshops known to stock
vistas of desolation: long hills,
swamps, barren sand, the bone-white
charm of a lost wallet.
I like the fresher breeze,
the way you lift up your hands
and tell me you know where you are.

All this we burned or traded. The bills,
the paycheques. A stereo speaker, the new dishwasher.
A radio, always present like a limp body
at the bottom of one of the meaner lakes.
I should be grateful for the noise, the smell of gas.
If you're smart you'll dowse yourself in it
as if that was all there was…

But that wasn't enough – we moved
off College, just north of the noise
trying to make sense of, not regret, exactly,
its copper trap, but the way a fluke bull's-eye
in a dirty pub slipped by unproved.
It has its attractions, but.

We flicked our butts and later
crossed the whole thing out.

NOTES ON A THEME

The theme of this party is the Old Masters
    and I'm the spitting image of Led Zeppelin.
The theme of this party is the future
    and I arrive like a crass proposition.
The theme of this party is keg stands
    and the boys all want to tap your ass.
The theme of this party is *Weekend at Bernie's*
    so we all come as Guildenstern and/or Rosencrantz.

The theme of this party is Alexander Graham Bell
    so I come as a footnote to his Wikipedia entry.
The theme of this party is body shots –
    as I drink I age hideously.
The theme of this party is mummification
    and my date is your Facebook account.
The theme of this party is commencement speeches;
    luckily I have a tattoo of the Sermon on the Mount.

The theme of this party is National Masturbation Month
    so I paper the tree of myself in tissue.
The theme of this party is childhood role models
    and I'm the unspeakable off-screen deeds of Scooby-Doo.
The theme of this party is running on empty
    and I'm the P.R. firm for a commercial organ harvest.
The theme of this party is Catholic
    and I dress like an ex–altar boy's therapist.

The theme of this party is catholic
    ergo we take a little E and smoke weed.
The theme of this party is making amends
    so I ground up your debts and bake you bread.
The theme of this party is transparency
    so I wear panties made of snow.
The theme of this party is the digital age
    and I'm pleasuring myself with a fibre optic dildo.

The theme of this party is authenticity
    so I sketch your portrait as an emoticon.
The theme of this party is the present;
    I'm a plane kissing your Pentagon.
The theme of this party is quietude
    and I swaddle an infant hangover.
The theme of this party is a slouching beast
    that drops, crawls on all fours.

The theme of this party is awful beer
    so we play it through a French horn.
The theme of this party is to come as you are
    thus I fashion a crown from Courtney Love's tax return.
The theme of this party is meaningless 'love'
    and I come as Thomas Kinkade.
The theme of this party is 'meaningless' love
    and I suck on the straw in your milkshake.

The theme of this party is poems about stars
    and I come dressed as a hard-on.
The theme of this party is heavy metal
    so I etch a tableau of my death in iron.
The theme of this party is modern medicine
    and it's generously sponsored by LASIK.
The theme of this party is the Real
    and we're just trying to keep it.

The theme of this party is bringing home the bacon
    so I wear an apron to the bloodbath.
The theme of this party is the industrial age
    and you come in dressed like a trainwreck.
The theme of this party is feeling shitty –
    I'm dressed as the cliffs of Dover.
The theme of this party is the fun we've had –
    I'm a dissertation on Schopenhauer.

The theme of this party is the fun we have
    so I set my disappointment to Auto-Tune.
The theme of this party is animal morality
    and I'm Matthew Arnold in a tiger costume.
The theme of this party is When in Rome;
    you've brought a lighter, I've dressed as a fiddle.
The theme of this party is a zygote,
    and we agree to split it down the middle.

The theme of this party is Indians and cowboys
    but I'm home with the pox.
The theme of this party is the miracle of flight
    and my costume's your little black box.

BIG SIGHS

What's not to like? Days coast in
and then coast out on a frothy surf,
as if surfing from one foam latté
to the next were the good life.
If coasting's got us this far, then surely
the truncated garden hose dangling
from a gas tank like a necktie
will get us the rest of the way.

Up here in the rafters – and stop me
if you've heard this one – I've staged
a small pageant to sort our various passions.
The resemblance to a smokestack is uncanny,
obnoxious, an accordion that hugs

its inner turmoil and wheezes.
What a production, music,
how it works you like a pro.
And by *you* I mean me,
and by *me* I mean I've tried to be good
to you in my own way, carried
you with me like a flask in your time of need.
You with your airplane heart and me,
a bad mechanic, leaving a wrench
like an extra bone in your landing gear.
You're so cute by the light of the evening news,
fuselage scattered desperately across a stretch of asphalt
like sun-starved foreigners on a beach.
Oh, the bodies of sweat that drip from us.

COUNTRY LIVING

It's all in your head, the articles say,
your life slanting at weird afternoon angles
against which you bump your head. Then the sudden bloom,
a second spring, and your noggin swells like interest rates.
It's not easy to live like this, but it's doable.

A friend stops by. He's sad, so you buy him a beer
and he tells you some things.
Then he gets on a train and leaves town for a while,
but it's still summer, there are people out.
Some of them are pretty, their skin tanned.

They're sweating – as are you – as if greasing their way
through popsicle season. In tongue-bath weather,
couples drive out to the country to hold hands.
It's not that I'm lonely, your friend had said,
but the hayloft of his brain behaves otherwise.

SMALL-TOWN BANK

Look, pinball, my Clementine,
    this is gonna ricochet all wrong
but one moment can't always account
    for another.
Cobble together your looser sentiments
into something approaching a lean-to,
or at least what a lean-to
    stands for.
Hope the colour of sea foam
                gives its address
    as a back alley. How am I
supposed to know which mailbox
    to leave its bank statement in?

DINOSAUR PORN

Things have names we learn and repeat:
Missionary, Cowgirl, Double Lutz
with a Half-Corkscrew Finish and a Fist Pump
for the Cameras. What's not to love
but the gesture we're used to?
                                So the stripmall
touches itself. A couple of punk kids
rush the adult video store, lily-white
hand-rolled cigarettes hinged to their lips.
Sixteen, maybe seventeen, old enough
to slip wrist-deep up a skirt at a stoplight
and think, *Finger like the clutch.*
And now, fingers under a sweater like a gun's
blunt point, roughly clubbing the clerk
with a slab of dumb violence.
                                They grab what they can.
Naturally, *Dinosaur Porn* is an attractive choice:
a man in a foam T. Rex outfit delivers pizza
to an all-girls college dorm. And when the kids
rush out, hands full of vhs tits and a wad of cash,
they broadside a promotional cardboard cutout
of the man-lizard – his green penis condom-capped
and jutting out like a tongue about to speak –
and topple him face-down on the carpet,
snout crumpled like a snail spooning itself in its shell.
One cardboard claw grips the floor, as if the porn star
is trying to crawl on all fours back to his apartment
where he'll thread the film of himself through a vcr
and unravel. At the end of the day, don't we all want
to unzip the animal suit and slosh drippingly to shore?

CONVENIENCE STORE

Quaint as a fax machine chugging
through lunch, the door chimes.
The fluorescents shiver and twitch,
like a button on a Nintendo controller
that's depressed and, sticky, just stays there.
In strip plazas everywhere
a procession of factories throws up.

A can of Dr. Pepper reproduces itself
deep in the aluminum vein. In the back
there are skids and skids and
skids of this shit and for years
someone just pushes them around.
I am replaceable. If you just don't care,
I think you know where your hands should be.

ACKNOWLEDGE YOUR SOURCES

It was a sky-draped year. We collected data like habits,
stockpiled information to have something to look into.
We were all about identity. Our primary theme was abstraction –

I know, right? With small words we touched it, and with big words
we brought it home. At a right-wing party's office, a bomb explodes.
At a leftist rally, something something. It was the year Heidegger

walked among us and seemed especially deep. Like, at the bottom.
A little red light signalled some really important shit.
As a gift to individualism, I eschewed the individual.

As a gift to myself, I learned to hail a cab like a flower
bending towards the newly departed. We kissed strangers,
stayed up late, depended on discipline to save the day.

That summer Justin Bieber insinuated himself into your heart
like an undercover agent. *The Insurgencies of Love* topped all
the charts. It was a good year for wanting and my stocks did well.

But you thought I'd gone all art deco in the mind
and the four-roomed apartment we'd claimed as ours
was a little too ... *something* for you.

You were raging for pastels. You wanted to move. So we spent
those eighteen months in a mid-sized European city whose transit
map, when crumpled, resembled a once-popular cognitive theory.

We tried to avoid cancer like the plague.
We wanted a sky the colour of a painting,
any painting, just something you don't have to *think* about.

One Saturday God went out, left us $20 for pizza
and said He'd be back in the morning.
The point was that we *could* have done anything.

Friends stood before us like a porchlight that night
and we fought over who would ring the doorbell.
You began writing letters to Jennifer Aniston

but in a really, like, political way.
As in, between two people.
Dear, no one's mind is right.

But then you left exactly how all the sad songs said you would
and I moved into a hotel the way a fastball chooses the mitt
it's tossed to: the glove's there and there's throwing to be done.

For a while, the world was everything in my suitcase.
The morning rose up like a Parisian mob, made unreasonable
demands, then settled in for an afternoon coffee. Or café, as they say.

In terms of currently accepted physics I was pretty fucking sad.
There were birds. I made my heart into the shape of the moon,
or perhaps it was the other way around,

but you must have seen my longing in the sky
because you came back. *God helps those He really likes,*
as Benjamin Franklin used to say.

I was coming down with something.
Beset with symptoms, I gave up style with panache.
That is: with panache, I gave up style. I tied my tie up tight.

Is there a doctor in the house? Drumroll, punchline, drumfill.
But, seriously, is there?
Because I'm finding it hard to breathe.

PARTY

This party is awesome. It's doped up. Def.
Dumb. I'm rocking this party like Sisyphus.
Broadly speaking, this party is an animal
that escapes from the zoo, has its photo captured
on the cover of several major newspapers
and is quietly euthanized a few weeks later.
Narrowly speaking, this party is as novel as a new tattoo.
Parliamentary democracy, journalistic responsibility
and this party: these are the pillars that hold society up
like a bandit. With its mickey of vodka and dayglo heart,
this party embodies seven fun facts about fun.

By a bed of roses this party lays me down. Its hand
at my belt. This party tugs gently.

PROVE TO ME YOU'RE NOT A ROBOT

People are so boring, though I shouldn't say so.
The great sea in their eyes, the keel and transom of them.
It wouldn't be fair to be all, *No,* you're *a ship in the night,*

but you get the drift. The flash and yearn of an Old Navy ad
with the look of the smell of a beach, but without an ocean
of dead things. No living things either, just the tranquil

Photoshop glow of Fun, a vigorous set of pearly whites,
a zombie-like satisfaction dressed in a laboriously starched collar
as if what counts for brains around here is a well-stitched button-up.

I confess to a sense of others as stimulus.

But, really, let's say I follow the laws of my various wants,
the here, the now, ache of boredom like a rotten tooth ...
testimony of the self as fuzzy and charming as a three-gin glow.

But this is all just pop solipsism. I know you're there. I just don't care.
Your overbite, your participation in assorted sample sizes.
Like I said: there's a great yawning gap, a heavy yawn.

There is yawning going on.
I'm thinking of what your inner life means to me:
faint scuttle below the deck, a quick hitch untied. I'm off.

SONG OF THE THINGS I'VE DONE

In this, the International Year of Wealth Management,
I had a fever about to break like a promise.
I spent my money wisely. The banks shivered, snapped,
spent a few months in a cast and emerged pale and new.

I insisted on actual rain in the claymation video.
I lingered in the committee room. When singing was needed,
I sung. I wrote a book on the new slang –
summary: the rigging's faulty, the lighting all wrong.

Night squeezed my shoulder and said,
Good shift, son. I looked up at the stars, gathered them in
like a shepherd gathers his flock before dinner.
I spent my money wisely. I ate well.

STAGE DIRECTIONS: EXEUNT, WITH FLOURISH

There's the bullet and then the bullet
hole, the victim and the school play's

death scene. There's the love poem
and then there's licking yourself clean.

Your couplet of visible ribs.
The brass charms that rattle around

your chest's hollow crib.
A rust-flecked reservoir, filling.

IL MIGLIOR FABIO

If you are what you eat then I
am the ass of a high school cheerleader,
high on boredom, behind the bleachers
after school. I am listening to robot rock at dawn
in a Ferrari made of glass. My body is hairless,
strong as OxyContin. I sweat oxytocin.
I gather the wind in my pipe and puff, puff.
I will not pass. I transpose your love song

from C-major to apathetic. The secret fifth chamber
of my heart weeps for your scoliosis,
but style does as style is, so I'll be cruising
the night with my gilded twelve-foot dick.
From my smithy I'll craft you a velvet half-hour.
I hope you catch my drift, emphasis *lick*.

ROY HALLADAY

'It's not fair.'
       – Aubrey Huff

Take life, whatever it is, one broken
    spoke at a time. Rosy-fingered
appendectomy, rusty five-day dawn.
       Look, we do what we can.
By we, I mean fans.
    I mean the Organization.
I mean the fingers
      required to throw a cutter.

Men want to be you –
      though that's not the point,
    men want to be everything –
but have you ever tried on a new pair of jeans
    and thought: I want this close to me?
  By you I mean: 8.0 IP 5 H 2 R 1 ER 3 BB 4 SO.
If something truly loves you
    it comes back with an inside fastball.

By you I mean a four-door family sedan,
    crack in the sunroof where the light
comes in. If you let something go and it
  loves you, it comes back at its shiny best.
I'm the worst kind of fair-weather
  love letter. Hubcap of need,
we're all out of polish
    and spit's not gonna work.

FAILURE

Dot-com speculation. Violin lessons.
Behind your old grade school, the spotty field
you first drank in.
                        No, *you're* son
has a failure to thrive. A train jumps its tracks
onto another, shittier set of tracks.
The spiny, thin-ribbed ego of success
takes a comparison to a condom personally.
Even though you meant it as a compliment.
And even though it's true.

CHERRY COLA

Dark can, glitzy stripper
on a victory lap, blunt smell of synthetics.
Heartbreak, heartbreak, someone
must have paid for this.

Nerves light like a spool of fishing thread.

Rodeo Clown, Drive-by Aspirations,
please wear name tags; I can never tell
which one has the runny nose
and which the funereal sense of humour.
Hold me tighter, Cherry
Cola. Stop letting go.

A BOY AT PINBALL

A boy plays pinball.
A boy grows flippers and a launch pad
and sets into still life:
A Flower Vase in Bar Lighting
or *A Fruit Basket Sets a New High Score.*

After school a boy leans his backpack against a wall,
gains open-water balance, glides out
to the shoal of himself and plays pinball.
From the machine emerges the art of recycling,
the vanishing magic of exchange:

quarters into the arcing free-float
of a silver ball in transit, his synapses'
snaky response. Translates his body
into points, points into proof of cause
and effect. If he were a game show
he would be the wheel in motion,
would call it *For Amusement Only.*
Would demonstrate with concision
what extends from the fingertips,
what, when tilted, complies.

A boy is a collision
careening through a light-up display
that halos his plate-glass reflection,
buoyant amid a garland of elastic bumpers.

His quarters a coin-box splash in the concluding
pool of transaction: wood and metal
and the lickity-split of buzzers,
points of contact flickering
in the slipstream of final score.

FOUND: PRE-ALPHA VERSION OF A BETTER SELF

For Andrew, depreciation offers
a range of modest savings: montage, composite image,
speak of a sausage in a frozen field.
The 1990s suggested Andrew's future
career: a country in the Eastern Bloc.
Of course, this was a little difficult.
Still, he dreamed and by 2001
he lifted the grey veil of place and exposed himself
in exhibition as a life-sized replica of the Cold War.
Known for its sensitive contexts,
it embodied years of time, care and thought.
Strictly speaking, no one was interested. The *L.A. Times* wrote:
'Rough and sketchy, Faulkner is a perfectionist
and very slow. His show, *Pre-alpha version*
of a better self, is a different sort of challenge
and its successes are few. The inability of even art students
to appreciate his practice is telling.
After twenty-five years the marks left are obvious,
the copyright a black-and-white of intention.'

PNEUMONIA

Lungs a tenement, swollen, easy to move into.
Hair-clogged, bathtub a standing pool.
The ground floor is sublet by a fevered tenant
who wallpapers with wet newspaper and wheatpaste.

Water slips through a valve's loosened fist. Drip.

A building of wood rot and mice, back alleys
cluttered with bone, shit, small bodies.
Lungs: welfare's small-change jar.
Plastic, whispery, just for now.

HALF-HITCH

A harbour in spring. Nice weather time.
Love takes to the air like a gull.
Beneath a tarpaulin sky,
cranes unload cargo like the hand of God
managing the world's chequing account.
A coroner fingers a gut's undigested bits.
At the stump of the dock a tourist centre
spills out another historical re-enactment –
this time, with feeling.

Fog squeezes between my chest's anvil
and the afternoon hammering down.
Once lodged in a body a bullet can drift for years.
You said you'd be here. Clinically speaking,
at least one of us is breathless.

RORSCHACH

What's stopping us from getting
what we want is unclear and frustratingly
good at what it does. A complex ecosystem
of trauma. The blotchy *What*
    in *What's wrong?*
  or *No, really, what's wrong?*
   When my quarter barricades
a gumball machine,
    I'll shake it for what's owed.

As an apparatus of joy, I do what I do.
Midday slump, don't you think
it's time you let go?

I'm more habit than gumption.
Once you realize change is infectious,
you dive right in.

On the hood of my car you swore
   you fell in love with metal.
     I'm dewy, damp with effort,
lurking in the middle distance.
 Hold me is an interpretive response
    to a battery of stimuli.
     My thoughts are guilty as charged:
Out There, context-free, wrangled in hazy
half-truth's attic light.

HEAD

A broken air pump
breathed into. Shoes spit-shined,
then scuffed. Hum and stitch,
a retro Singer. A pop-song hook.

Tracing paper. Practical
hydraulics. A river robbed
of its bed. The seventh-inning stretch.
A fist of reason wiggled free
like a Plinko chip.

No, wait, that's the heart.

REMOTE

What do you want me to say?
Like a bent wire I let radio signals
tie themselves about me.
The hearts of larger animals
signal intent like a high-wire act:
what's up there leaves us smitten
and then leaves us. In commercials
they always get it right the first time.

X-rays confirm our first suspicion: there are things
we should have done. At times I'm seized.
Like a minor sitcom character, I appear at the edge
of scenes. There are those who say love is a symptom
of the middle class, leather pants a symptom
of middle-class resentment. On the more remote
planets our laundry loses its studio crispness.
It's not a matter of trying harder.
Believe me. I've tried.

THE MOON

Clean, sharp, a knife stepping from the shower.
A pock-faced snowglobe without the snow.
Moon, stop peering through the sunroof of my Volvo.

When it humps, the moon insists you hump.
Bump in the belly of an ex, bump of an object
beneath your car. And when it cries out
like a wounded raccoon, who will collect

donations for its rehabilitation? You?
After several costly surgeries, the moon is still hideous,
but oh, the arc of its nightly touchdown pass.

From the First World's left ventricle I pump
my fist furiously for each small victory
while the moon circles back on itself:
notch another one for The End of History.

PASSENGER

This place is compact as a small-town convenience store,
cramped as a big city mayor's heart, car with its
clutch on the left and factory-leather cologne.
It's barely morning. A headline reads:

Study shows space in our cities declining
and several folks nod when a commuter train
shudders and halts. Slack as a punctured tire

we wait. It's late in the morning.
Across the Gardiner the sun walks from hood to hood.
Here on the island of office politics, everyone's basically

pretty nice to your face. After lunch I tinker in Excel
at the edges of The Great Office Poem.
The afternoon's light arrives like mail

through a door's small slot.
To say we are equal to what we do
is to lend a softer glow to the underground

parking garage. And then, on the hour, cars stutter
like a misplaced accent. We are always on our way home.
According to the radio: *from Avenue*

to the Don Valley. This little red wagon
won't pull itself. Sign as close as you can to the *x*
or adjust your expectations. It's deep into evening.

In the hundred or so metres of existence
a porchlight blinks off, then on.
It gets later and then it stays that way.

LIKE CANCER

In response to a common theme, my moustache grows.
Regarding irony, my moustache curls at its ends.
I walk, then I walk some more. Thus my days are filled.

It's true what they say: if you've been around the block
you know the block rather well. Billboards rise
like stubble. After a while, the block resembles
the middle distance in a high school art project.

I shave and I shave. Thus my washbasin is filled.
In response to my face, I weep and wonder.
The lines of your face
draw such pretty little pictures.

Sharpen your crayons, there's some shading to be done.
With gears dense as headaches we chug along.
Like cancer we're full of ourselves and make our own fun.

HANGOVER

Outside is a wet cigarette. Last night is
half ash, half scrambled porn.
I put what where? There's a dead rat
in my mouth. Teeth fuzzy,
fermented, near-victims of a flood
hauled up sputtering and waterlogged.

The morning crackles like the desert
between stations on the AM dial.
The stock market is one thing,
an op-ed on abolishing the penny another.
There's a recession lurking somewhere.
I'm out of Advil. I can't think of what to give up first.

AMEN

What's there can fit in a hand. Take, for example,
the lines in a hand that years have called forth.

You can't be around nothing, thank God. On an ocean
liner, people cling to one another. On an ocean liner,

people turn away. At the heart of the matter
a slow heart beats. I'm frothing at the bit.

Dear computer, please live one more year.

Minister of Loping Through One's Twenties
Like a Three-Legged Dog, I'd like to make a deposition:

I've slept in the tall grass while someone mowed
the lawn. Some days I wake up less, wake up missing,

knotted or stripped to the wire. Tell me anything
in your best foghorn voice and I'll believe you.

INCIDENTAL

I was a stranger in a dream. From a high window,
I looked down. A bass line with legs to its tits
and tits to its chin took a long walk out of town.
I was as lonely as the first Jew in America,
as the last dollar in a wallet.
Some nights I could drown in fun.
This is about the economy adrift as a kid
in his dad's suit. It's a wide-open continent
and the Kool-Aid here's the best.
This is about what just happened.
This is about what's next.

WALK HOME, EARLY MORNING

The air, leaned on.
An unfinished pillar,
a suburban basement
hungry for plumbing.

Sleep a lazy hook
winching you forward.

Chain-link fences cut cookies
from a doughy sky.
The moon rattles along,
a fat child with a stick
and a blooming appetite.

A radio with a bent antenna
tracks light crossing state lines.

A bottle, pissed in,
is a movement toward
clarity – like you, reclined
against a brick wall,
trying not to spill.

And the day kicks it over,
sunny and dumb. An AM station's
call sign circles the vandal
like a squad car.

Hello, caller, and welcome
to the show.

NOTES AND ACKNOWLEDGEMENTS

Some of these poems have appeared in *Arc Poetry Magazine*, *Dinosaur Porn* (Ferno House/The Emergency Response Unit, 2010), *The Fiddlehead*, *Ottawater*, *The Puritan*, *This Magazine*, The Week Shall Inherit the Verse, Toronto Poetry Vendors, *Wascana Review*, and the *Windsor Review*, as well as the chapbooks *Useful Knots and How to Tie Them* (The Emergency Response Unit, 2008) and *Mean Matt and Other Shitty People* (Ferno House, 2012). Thanks to all who produced these publications.

Thanks to the Ontario Arts Council and the Toronto Arts Council for their generous support.

'That's what she said' is for Leigh Nash.

'This time with feeling' and 'Big sighs' owe a debt to Christian Hawkey's poem 'Up here in the rafters everything is clear' (*The Book of Funnels*, Verse Press, 2004).

'Found: The smell of gas' is a cento of lines taken from a number of Canadian poets.

'Notes on a theme' is after a line by the band The Hold Steady.

All the text in 'Found: Pre-alpha version of a better self' appeared in various forms on andrewfaulkner.com and the now-defunct andrew-faulkner.net and andrewfaulkner.co.uk.

'Head' is after a poem by Jeramy Dodds.

High fives to everyone at Coach House for their endless big-hearted work. Big hugs to family for their support, especially Jean, Steve and Ben.

Thanks to Spencer Gordon, Mat Laporte, Elisabeth de Mariaffi, Jeff Latosik, Aaron Tucker and Nicholas Lea for comments and advice on earlier drafts of the manuscript. And thanks to Dionne Brand, Karen Solie and my classmates and faculty for thoughtful readings of my work throughout my time in the University of Guelph's MFA in Creative Writing program.

Thanks to Kevin Connolly for early edits and encouragement. Thanks to Jeramy Dodds for his sharp and tireless eye, and unerring insight.

Last but biggest thanks to Leigh, my first and best reader, for her love, large brain and unwavering attention to detail.

ABOUT THE AUTHOR

ANDREW FAULKNER co-curates The Emergency Response Unit, a chapbook press. His poems have been published in *The Best Canadian Poetry in English 2011*, and his chapbook *Useful Knots and How To Tie Them* was shortlisted for the bpNichol Chapbook Award.

Typeset in Aragon and Aragon Sans, from Canada Type.

Printed at the old Coach House on bpNichol Lane in Toronto, Ontario, on Zephyr Antique Laid paper, which was manufactured, acid-free, in Saint-Jérôme, Quebec, from second-growth forests. This book was printed with vegetable-based ink on a 1965 Heidelberg kord offset litho press. Its pages were folded on a Baumfolder, gathered by hand, bound on a Sulby Auto-Minabinda and trimmed on a Polar single-knife cutter.

Edited by Jeramy Dodds
Designed by Alana Wilcox
Cover art by Masahiro Sato

Coach House Books
80 bpNichol Lane
Toronto ON M5s 3J4
Canada

416 979 2217
800 367 6360

mail@chbooks.com
www.chbooks.com